Pebble™ Plus

Healthy Eating with MyPyramid
Drinking Water

by Mari C. Schuh

Consulting Editor: Gail Saunders-Smith, PhD

Consultant: Barbara J. Rolls, PhD
Guthrie Chair in Nutrition
The Pennsylvania State University
University Park, Pennsylvania

Capstone
press
Mankato, Minnesota

Pebble Plus is published by Capstone Press,
151 Good Counsel Drive, P.O. Box 669, Mankato, Minnesota 56002.
www.capstonepress.com

1 2 3 4 5 6 11 10 09 08 07 06

Library of Congress Cataloging-in-Publication Data
Schuh, Mari C., 1975–
    Drinking water / by Mari C. Schuh.
    p. cm.—(Pebble Plus. Healthy eating with MyPyramid)
    Summary: "Simple text and photographs present information about drinking water and ways to drink
enough water"—Provided by publisher.
    Includes bibliographical references and index.
    ISBN-13: 978-0-7368-5375-0 (hardcover)
    ISBN-10: 0-7368-5375-8 (hardcover)
    1. Water in the body—Juvenile literature. 2. Water—Metabolism—Juvenile literature. 3. Thirst—Juvenile
literature. I. Title. II. Series.
QP535.H1S38 2006
613.2'87—dc22
                      2005031200

Credits
Jennifer Bergstrom, designer; Kelly Garvin, photo researcher; Stacy Foster, photo shoot coordinator

Photo Credits
Capstone Press/Karon Dubke, cover, 1, 5, 7, 10–11, 13, 15, 16–17, 19
Corbis/Ariel Skelley, 21; Duomo, 8–9

The author dedicates this book to her friend Delorna Marti of North Mankato, Minnesota.

**The U.S. Department of Agriculture (USDA) does not endorse any products, services,
or organizations.**

Note to Parents and Teachers

The Healthy Eating with MyPyramid set supports national science standards related to
nutrition and physical health. This book describes and illustrates drinking water. The
images support early readers in understanding the text. The repetition of words and
phrases helps early readers learn new words. This book also introduces early readers
to subject-specific vocabulary words, which are defined in the Glossary section. Early
readers may need assistance to read some words and to use the Table of Contents,
Glossary, Read More, Internet Sites, and Index sections of the book.

Table of Contents

Water and Your Body

Are you thirsty?

Did you drink

lots of water today?

Most of your body

is made of water.

Your body needs water

every day.

Everything your body
does on the inside
depends on water.
Water helps all your
body parts work right.

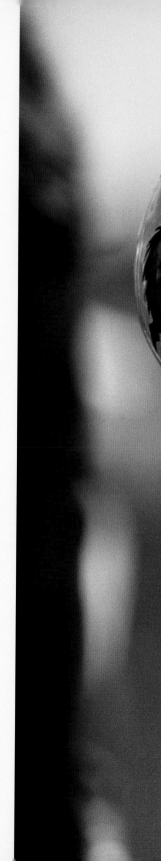

Your body needs water
to help digest food.
Water also helps your body
get rid of waste.

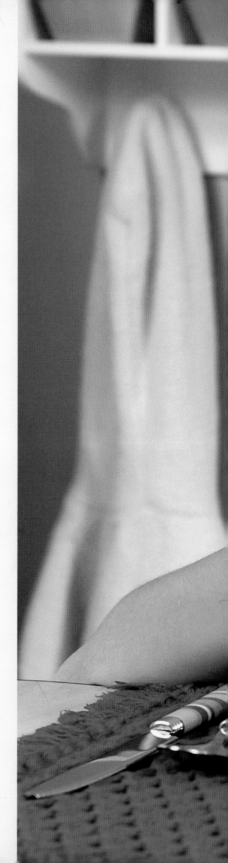

When You Need Water

You lose water

when you play and sweat.

Take water breaks.

Gulp, gulp, gulp.

13

Drink plenty of water
when you're sick.
If your body doesn't
have enough water,
it won't work its best.

Enjoying Water

You can bring water
wherever you go.
Bring bottles of water
along to the park.

You can get some water
from the food you eat.
Soup, fruits, and vegetables
have lots of water. Enjoy!

19

You feel good when you
drink enough water.
Now it's time to play!

Glossary

digest—to break down food so it can be absorbed into your blood and used by your body

sweat—having a salty liquid come out through the pores in your skin because you are hot or nervous

thirsty—needing or wanting water or another liquid

waste—food and water that your body does not use or need after food has been digested

Read More

Kalz, Jill. *Water.* Healthy Me. Mankato, Minn.: Smart Apple Media, 2003.

Kerley, Barbara. *A Cool Drink of Water.* Washington, D.C.: National Geographic Society, 2002.

Royston, Angela. *Water and Fiber for a Healthy Body.* Body Needs. Chicago: Heinemann, 2003.

Internet Sites

FactHound offers a safe, fun way to find Internet sites related to this book. All of the sites on FactHound have been researched by our staff.

Here's how:

1. Visit *www.facthound.com*

2. Type in this special code **0736853758** for age-appropriate sites. Or enter a search word related to this book for a more general search.

3. Click on the **Fetch It** button.

FactHound will fetch the best sites for you!

Index

Word Count: 139
Grade: 1
Early-Intervention Level: 13